Become a Successful freelancer - Step by Step
Taught by a Canadian employer with over 1000 projects and 15 years of offshore experience.

By: Lior Izik

How to use this course:

This course will turn you into a special resource. The lessons here are designed to teach you exactly what Western employers want, helping you stand out from thousands of other offshore workers.

The first time you read this course, you should take no action. Read the lessons, but do not complete any exercises. When you read through the course for the second time, finish all homework exercises in full detail.

Some homework exercises are meant for offshore workers with existing clients in North America or Europe. Ignore these if you are new to freelancing in the West.

Each small homework section will come together in the end to create a business plan. This will become your working plan, to be followed before, during, and after all projects.

Introduction:

My name is Lior Izik and I live in Toronto, Canada.

I have managed multiple IT companies in the fields of programming, design, and marketing. I have experience in web development, apps, security, sysadmin, databases, project management, call centers, QA, and much more.

I have been working with offshore resources for over 15 years. Thousands of projects have taken me to many different countries, including India, China, Pakistan, and Bangladesh. I've moved millions of dollars from my bank account paying offshore developers, and worked in areas that most people have never heard of.

In total, I have worked on over 1000 projects with over 800 different resources. Some of these projects were successes, and others were disasters. Some finished on time, and some are still waiting to be launched today. There were many times where I told myself: "This is the last time I am ever working with offshore resources - it will never work!" I had many resources stop talking to me for days, keeping me up at night wondering what was going on with my project.

During those 15 years, I tried everything I could think of to attract quality offshore resources. I built my own development centers in Ukraine, India and Bangladesh, paid bonuses, gave penalties, and worked with every online hiring platform that was available. I really have tried it all.

This course will summarize my 15 years of experience working with offshore teams and freelancer individuals. Companies in North America and Europe are currently looking for offshore resources with the knowledge and skills outlined in this course. The more you fit the profile, the easier it will be for you to be hired and retain customers in the future. If you study this course and follow its lessons carefully, I am sure you will be very successful.

Lesson 1 - Know Your Employer

The first thing I want you to do is imagine your current or future employer's life from their point of view. In order to serve your employer in the best possible way, you need to know exactly who he is, what makes him comfortable, and what he expects from you.

There are 2 main reasons why companies hire offshore resources:
1. **The company wants to save money.** It is less expensive to use offshore developers.
2. **The company is missing talent.** A specific skillset is needed for a project, but isn't available locally, so the company must hire offshore.

In both cases, the employer is expecting someone who merges well with his existing team. They want someone who feels like an onshore employee working from home.

As human beings, we like to work with people who are similar to us. This means that you need to understand how people think and act in Europe and North America. I'm not saying that one way of thinking is better than the other, just that people feel most comfortable around what they're used to.

You can do things to make your employer more comfortable working with an offshore employee. There are many things that will merge people together in these situations. Sharing the same language, hobby, profession, sports team, weather - the list goes on. Focus on the things you have in common, and it will pay off in the long run.

The culture in North America and Europe is about making money, and having a comfortable life. There is an entire industry dedicated to pleasure and getting things done as easily as possible, and this is ultimately what your employer is looking for.

For many companies, money is everything, and their owners don't care about your family or your personal life. They see you as a resource that gets paid to deliver work. You are part of a business transaction that they need to make, and that is all there is to it.

Because of this, any action that costs the business owner money or makes his job harder will get you in trouble. This is a key point that you need to remember before we proceed any further, as this course includes a number of lessons related to this idea. If you can save your employer money and help them work less, you will be a star resource.

In North America and Europe, we have something called "credit." Credit is a core concept that we base our lives on. If you want a loan to buy a house in the West, the bank checks your "credit score" before they give it to you. This credit score reflects your financial history, and worsens when you do something bad. In the West, it is important to have a good credit score, as there are very few financial opportunities available if you don't.

You must treat your relationship with your employer as though you were managing a credit score. When you're hired for a project by someone new, you start with a neutral credit rating. As you continue to work with your employer, your score worsens or improves depending on how you act. If you deliver what your employer wants, your score increases. Your score drops when you take too much time off, miss deadlines, fail to complete tasks, lie, skip meetings, or produce low-quality work. If your score drops too far, you will be replaced. Part of what this course will teach you is how to build a high credit score in the eyes of your employer.

"Small talk" is another important part of North American and European culture. It is common to make "small talk" about small things like weather, sports, local news, and traffic before getting into business.

Small talk is part of the way people in the West function, but I have never had this connection with an offshore resource because our lives are so different. It is difficult to relate to the daily life of someone from a very different culture. There is nothing to talk about except the project you're working on together.

I personally do not match the profile of a very social person, but I recognize that most people around me appreciate small talk. I see small talk as a glue that connects people, so I make the effort. If you take 10 minutes each day to read the news from the country that your employer lives in, you will have all you need to get some small talk going. A short 1-3 minute conversation is all it will takes to make them feel comfortable. If they are not engaging you in conversation, then they are probably not interested in small talk, and you can ignore this step.

Another thing to keep in mind is that most people in the West are not practicing religion multiple times throughout the day. If you are someone who prays a few times each day, you should not report that to your employer. It will be hard for them to understand. Instead, just take the time you need without mentioning exactly where you're going. Announcing your religion shows him how you are different, rather than what you have in common. Remember, the more your employer sees you doing things from his culture, the more he will want to connect with you - it's just the way people function.

Names in the West are much different than those in the East. Like an actor choosing a catchy "stage name," you should pick a name that is very easy for your Western employer to pronounce. I am not saying to go by a Western name, as it probably won't sound right. I once spoke with an offshore resource from India who identified himself as "John," and it sounded so wrong that it was alarming. Instead of replacing your name, simplify it for Western speakers. If your name is "Aishwarya," then call yourself "Aish" at work. The name is easy to pronounce, and is still partially yours.

As an employer, I am always excited to see an offshore resource who is engaged in the project. So how do you show that you're engaged? Tell your employer that in order to produce the best possible results in the upcoming project, you would like to know more about their business. Showing interest in your employer's company is a very good thing to do. Of course, you can't ask how much money he generates each month, but you can ask about his main services, his most popular products, and whether the market they work is local or international. Any general business questions will make you look good.

You must know your employer. The more you seem like an onshore employee, the better. If your employer is comfortable with you, you will enjoy longer contracts and more job offers.

HOMEWORK:

1. Create a list of things you can change about yourself to make your employer more comfortable based on this lesson.

2. List all of the reasons you lost projects or employers in the past. The more you dive into the past, the more you can learn about your future. Catching mistakes now helps you avoid them later.

3. Find the name of your employer's native country or city. Find 5 news items related to this area. Read only the highlights - details are not important.

4. Choose your "stage name." Modify your name, don't replace it.

Lesson 2 - Be Better Than Your Competition

Becoming better than your offshore competition is not going to be difficult. You have already invested in improving your professional career by purchasing this course. Absorbing a few lessons from this program will make you 100-times better than your average competition.

It's important to understand that you don't need to be the best in the world. Consider this story:

Two friends are walking in the African Savanna when they spot a hungry lion on the prowl. One of the friends immediately unties his shoes and rips them off of his feet.

"What are you doing?" asks his friend.

"I'm going to run," replies the shoeless man.

"Do you think that you can run faster than a lion?"

"No, but I can definitely run faster than you!" replies the shoeless man, then sets off running at full speed.

Keep this story in mind as you continue to invest in your professional career. You do not need to be the best in the world to get business. You just need to be better than the other offshore resources being interviewed for the position.

Right now, as you sit reading this course, know that there are millions of other offshore workers who aren't making the same effort. Every lesson you read here will put you one step ahead of your competition. Soon, they'll be far behind you.

It's important to be thinking at all times how you can be better than the competition around you. Using what you've learned from this course, try to look for mistake they make, and avoid repeating them yourself. This is a very important lesson that you will need to remember moving forward.

Imagine that an employer is interviewing five offshore marketing resources from Bangladesh. Four of them have not read this course, and they answer the employer's questions in the same way. The fifth resource understands what the employer is looking for. When the employer asks him the same questions, the fifth employer answers in a way that makes the interviewer think: "Wow, this guy is one of us."

Who do you think will get the job?

HOMEWORK:

1. Open your internet browser and visit Google.com. Make sure that you are on this exact site, not the Google for your country. Search for "common interview questions." Learn what questions you need to prepare for and write down your responses. Keep your answers - you will be using them again later in the course.

2. Look closely at the people you work with. List 3 mistakes you see your coworkers making based on what you have learned in the first 2 lessons. Think of how you would do things differently, and write down your solution.

Lesson 3 - Ask Questions, Be Understood

One of the key problems I have experienced with offshore resources is their lack of understanding, something usually caused by their unwillingness to ask questions when something isn't clear.

Other times, it is caused by language issues. If I ask someone in North America or Europe whether they can finish a project by next week, and they say "Okay," I will assume that they have confirmed that the work will be done on time. However, in the mind of the offshore employee, "Okay" means "I hear you." The employee is not committing to the deadline, they are just trying to acknowledge that they understand what was said. As you can imagine, this is a big problem for your employer. Do not answer "Okay" to a Western employer's request unless you fully understand what is being said, and can meet the deadline being requested.

After deadlines kept being missed and tasks continued to be performed incorrectly, I eventually asked my offshore resource what the problem was. What went wrong? Why didn't you ask more questions when I asked whether or not you understood what I was saying? There were rare cases where the developer would answer me honestly, and tell me: "I was afraid that you would fire me if I asked too many questions!"

One of the most important lessons I can pass on to you that asking questions is good for you in every way. How, you ask?

Here are a few reasons how asking questions helps you:
1. As I mentioned in lesson 1, Western employers value offshore resources who ask questions, because it shows that they are engaged with the project and care about its success.
2. Asking questions is the only way to truly understand what is expected of you. If you do not know exactly what your employer wants, you will never be able to deliver results that satisfy him.

3. Even if you feel as though you have done everything right, it is worthwhile to ask questions. Reviewing the tasks with your employer will show that you are committed, and impress them with your understanding.
4. The worst offshore resources are those who don't ask questions, because those are the employees that deliver bad work or miss deadlines. You can avoid losing money and clients with failed tasks by simply asking questions.

HOMEWORK:

1. Select one of your past projects and review your communications with the employer. You can look over your Google Talk history, email threads, Skype chat log, or any other recorded communication. Check to see if any tasks were misunderstood, and note how your employer reacted. You will only have to see this pattern play out once, and you will never make this mistake again.

2. Write down the procedure of handling project questions.

3. Write down the procedure of handling "kickoff meetings." Kickoff meetings take place once you are hired for a project, giving you an opportunity to go over everything that needs to be done.

Lesson 4 - Know Your Strengths, and Stick to Them

I once worked with an offshore contractor on an HTML5 project that turned out great. I couldn't have asked for better service, and the end result was of very good quality. I had no complaints, and even offered the developer a bonus.

Once the project finished, the contractor asked me if any other projects were available. I told him that I had no more HTML5 work, but mentioned there were always projects in the pipeline.

The developer insisted that he could handle any web project that I had. He assured me that he had lots of experience. At that point, we had enjoyed a great 3-month relationship, and I had no reason not to trust him. I hired him to build a PHP Cake website.

The PHP Cake website I had in mind was very simple, and would take no more than 2 weeks to complete. After a week, I could already tell that the work being done was of low quality. I quickly realized that I was a victim of the "Know It All" problem.

When I spoke to the developer about the problems I saw, he assured me that he would fix everything in a few days. By now, we had already missed the deadline, and now we were falling behind even further. I offered to work with him to solve whatever issues he was having, but he insisted that he could complete the job on his own. It seemed that he was too embarrassed to ask questions.

A week later, the final result came in, and though the work had improved, it was still far from what was supposed to be delivered. I closed the project on bad terms, and dismissed this developer. I gave him a negative review, and withheld payment because the product was not delivered as promised.

What can we learn from this story?

If the developer would have known his strengths and stuck to them, he would have gotten many more jobs from me in the future. With a few clients like me, the developer could have had a lifetime's worth of projects and income. As an "expert" in HTML5, he would have been in a position to raise his fees over time.

Instead, he tried to take on a project that he was unqualified to handle, and lost a paying client as a result. The developer also wasted 3 weeks for nothing, as he was not paid for the late and low-quality work he submitted.

After 15 years working with offshore resources from many different countries, I got the feeling that professionals operated in very different ways from culture to culture. In North America, companies build their vendor lists based on positive experiences, and maintain these relationships for a very long time. Building a positive relationship between vendor and company owner is the main focus - they are building a "credit score" as we discussed in Lesson 1.

However, I have witnessed many offshore resources that seem to be working towards a very different goal. Rather than building a good credit score and positive relationship with their employer, I get the feeling that their only goal is to make quick money. Some offshore resources don't seem to care what happens next, so long as they are paid for the project in front of them.

I am sure that this is not actually the goal of the offshore resources that I work with, but that is the feeling that I get sometimes as an employer. To prevent your employer from feeling this way, it is very important to find ways to build positives experiences. If you are not proficient in a specific field, don't take the job, or you will probably create a very negative experience that costs you money and clients.

If you do want to work on a project in an unfamiliar field, be honest with your employer. Explain that this area is not your strength, but that you are willing to give it a try for a small amount. So long as you make an effort to communicate openly and honestly, things will work out well for you. Even lower-quality work can be acceptable so long as it meets your employer's expectations.

HOMEWORK:

1. Create a list of all of your strong skills. The list should include every service that you are qualified to provide. Give yourself a grade or quality rating for each service, and include how many projects you have completed in this field.

   Once the list is complete, you will know exactly which services you can and cannot offer clients, and will not have to worry about burning relationships with Western employers.

2. Create a list of clients that you have lost due to the problem outlined in this section. Estimate how many years your work relationship could have lasted if you had stuck to your strengths, and how much money could have been made in that time.

3. Decide what your strongest skill is, and consider what would happen if you master that one small niche. There are many great employers out there looking for very specific resources, and mastering one skill can make you lots of money.

Lesson 5 - Be Honest

When working with offshore developers, honesty can be a big challenge. I've heard every excuse, from heart attacks to dogs eating laptops. Eventually, I had to stop believing what I was being told. After 15 years of lies and tall tales, I was motivated to create a YouTube video warning business owners about the dangers of overseas collaborations.

You can see that video here: https://www.youtube.com/watch?v=wGee4V7ejS4

As you can see, the video is quite popular. At the time that this course was being written, it had nearly 20,000 views and over 400 likes. The amount of attention this short and simple video has gotten confirms that many other business owners have been burned the same way.

I think that it's important to bring attention to this problem, and to the mistakes I've made. Understanding these bad experiences will help you avoid being part of the problem, and turn you into a special resource that no employer in their right mind would ever release.

You can tell your employer anything, but even the greatest excuse in the world won't matter. As I said in Lesson 1, Western culture is all about making money - if you miss deadlines and turn in low-quality work, you won't survive in this business.

An employer will appreciate the truth, no matter how bad it makes you look. The truth can be hard to tell, but it's always much better than a lie. Some things can be difficult to get across through language and cultural barriers, but always make the effort to tell the truth. It will pay off.

I had a unique case where an outrageous-sounding story turned out to be true, and my employee saved his job with an open and honest explanation. This employee disappeared on me for a full week, causing our project to be delayed. I saw him online one day and was ready to fire him. I said: "How could you go offline for a week when we had an important project to finish? We missed our deadline because of you." He explained to me that the internet in his village had gone down, and there was nothing he could do. He had even tried to visit a neighbouring village to contact me, but the internet was offline there too. I was not in his village or his culture, so I had trouble understanding how he could completely lose internet access, but luckily he made the effort to explain himself. The employee sent me a link to a news article about the internet crash, and when I read it using Google Translate I saw that he was telling the truth.

I valued his honesty so much that I kept him on the project, and continued to work with him for many years. I still remember this interaction because it was so rare to get an honest answer, especially one that sounded so much like an excuse. It was a nice change from the stories I usually hear.

I had many offshore workers tell me that they were working on my project night and day, but then I would see them being very active on freelancer platforms. Are you really going to tell me that I have your full focus when I see you bidding constantly on projects from other clients?

I will spy on an offshore resource long enough to verify that they are doing what I suspect them of, and then release them for good. Your Western employer will do the same, which is another reason why it's best to be honest. Of course, if I'm at a point where I'm having to keep tabs on you, you're already halfway out the door.

From the employer's perspective, you should understand that it is very costly to release an employee. In fact, it costs the employer more than the employee. It is important for you to understand both sides of this scenario fully. I will touch on this further in this course, and fully explain what happens to the employer when a project crashes.

From the employee's perspective, however, I understand that many of these excuses are not given with the intention of deceiving me or stealing my money. Many times, an offshore worker will take on too many projects at once, overestimate their proficiency in a certain area, be kept waiting by unresponsive friends who offered to help, and so on - in other words, they had the best intentions, but circumstance has left them in a bad spot. Now, they're left in a situation where they have little to say to their employer, other than excuses for why work wasn't finished.

The best approach is to start with the truth, and to communicate with your client as often as possible. Update them on things whether they are good or bad. You basically want to communicate with them in the way I hope you do with your family. If your wife sends you to buy bread and you can't find a loaf, you don't disappear on her until you find one. She will assume the worst. You don't lie to her either, because that definitely won't end well. It is the same thing with your employer - even if there is no "news" or serious progress, you need to give them updates. Staying in contact and communication with your employee will reduce their stress by reassuring them that you are on top of the project. When your employer knows you're in charge, he can work less. Remember Lesson 1 - if you can help your employer spend less money and work less, you rise to the top of the list of offshore resources!

HOMEWORK:
1. Write down every story or excuse you've ever told your clients, and list the reasons for each.

2. Review your list. For each item, try to think of what you could have said in this scenario, and imagine how your honesty would have worked for you.

Lesson 6 - Difficult Times Ahead

Low-quality offshore workers are making it harder for their professional peers to be taken seriously. The mistakes of others can hurt your chances as more Western employers lose faith in offshore work - there may be difficult times ahead.

After experiencing some of the problems I have outlined in the previous lessons, many employers I know have begun to rethink whether or not hiring offshore is the right move. Large companies funding offshore development centers and small business owners hiring individual offshore resources have scaled back their offshore hiring after facing problems in 2014 and 2015.

Employers want to reduce their costs, but not at the expense of quality work. For Western employers, it isn't worth hiring offshore resources to save money if the final product is not good. If your employers submit low-quality work, they end up losing paying clients, and costing themselves more than they save by hiring overseas workers.

Consider the following example:

I have a client who sends me one job every month. Each project is worth an average of $5,000. At $5,000 per month, it means this client is worth $60,000 per year. Will it be wise for me to hire an offshore resource to handle one of this client's projects?

In my experience employing offshore workers, only 1 out of every 10 projects turns out well. When I say it turned out well, I mean it is delivered on-time and on-budget. Based on those odds, that means that I have a 90% chance of burning my client by delivering a project that is late, low-quality, or over-budget. If my client gets a poor result, they will take their business elsewhere. That means hiring an offshore employee could potentially cost me $60,000 per year - much more than I could hope to save by hiring overseas.

This is the way I see big companies and small business employers thinking about offshore resources. Only once you truly understand how the other side thinks can you begin to match their expectations.

There are many other reasons why business owners have begun migrating away from hiring offshore. Here is another example:

Imagine an offshore marketing company advertising that they can promote any site so that it ranks in Google's top-10 search listings. This is an extremely common offer that you'll see offshore marketers making, and it hurts the reputation of honest offshore workers in the world.

Of course, if you think about it for a moment you'll understand that this claim is impossible - if it were true, they would create sites with main keywords, rank in the top-10, and then sell pay-per-click for big money. Since the offer is not real, 80% of their clients disappear right away and write a bad review about the company. Now there are terrible reviews warning people who want to work with offshore marketing companies.

Those clients who continued working with these offshore marketers end up getting burned badly. They lose money with no result, and if the company used unethical means of promotion, the client's entire website will be crushed with penalties, losing all of its positions. The client warns all of his fellow employers not to use offshore marketing resources.

This offshore marketing company didn't have to be part of the problem. Some offshore marketers are professional and honest, and will provide quality marketing based on proven Google strategy. They maintain clients for a long time on a monthly basis. They follow the lessons from previous section, easily building strong reputations and securing repeat business.

I am a big believer in the offshore marketing, and love each of my team members as a brother. The problem is that I had to burn through 800 low-quality employees over 15 years to find the 60 that I love and trust. If I took the same 800 projects to Canadian companies, I would probably have a list of 600 quality resources to work with.

I want to see more offshore resources succeed, and believe that this course can help. By absorbing the lessons I present in this course, offshore employees can reverse the negative migration that is currently in effect, and restore Western employers' faith in overseas workers.

HOMEWORK:

1. Stop the negative migration that is costing offshore workers job opportunities. Spread the ideas contained in this course. Together, we can change the way overseas resources operate, and how they are seen in the eyes of Western employers.

Lesson 7 - Marketing Yourself Properly

Whether you are a freelancer or the owner of a huge company, you will need to advertise your services. Unfortunately, this is not an easy task. The competition is fierce. Hundreds of thousands of people from all over the world are competing for a limited number of offshore positions. How are you going to stand out?

There are many marketing tools available to you. Some are more effective than others when advertising in the Western world. Let's discuss your options:

1. **Google Adwords (pay per click)** - This approach is very expensive if you're trying to compete in North America and Europe. You can end up paying $15 per click and still have a very low chance of converting it to business. Eventually, you end up with a big bill and no jobs. In today's market, only big companies can survive using Adwords.
2. **Build a website -** Having a website is a good idea. Make sure that you have a portfolio so that a potential employer can see samples of your work. Include a few paragraphs about each project discussing how it went, the development time, name of your team, and so on. It is very important to include these paragraphs as a way of proving the work belongs to you. Many offshore resources use fake portfolios, and employers know this. Including reference information makes employers more likely to believe you.
3. **Create a profile on Elance and similar platforms -** It is very helpful to have a strong profile in an online freelancer community. Complete all sections and make sure the profile looks great. Ask one of your clients to take a look and give you honest feedback. Include your portfolio, some visuals, and a video interview if possible. If you have decent English, recording a quick video where you introduce yourself is a huge asset, helping you stand out to your employer as a person rather than just a name. Talk a bit about your personal life, and a lot about your professional career. Mention projects you've worked on, technologies you're familiar with, and so on. Remember the common interview questions you researched in Lesson 2? Answer them in this video

interview, speaking slowly and as clearly as possible. Make the interview up to 3 minutes long.

4. **Social media** - Social media networks will not do much for you. Don't spend your time on it.

5. **Google Organic** - This will not work if your office is offshore. A virtual address in North America or Europe may work for awhile, but Google will eventually remove it. Don't waste your time on this front. If you have strong content writers and an effective SEO process, you can compete on "SERVICE in CITY" keywords. For example, "HTML5 Developer in Dhaka" would work - though "HTML5 Developer in New York" will not!

6. **Maintain a blog** - Blogs can be effective, so long as you have something meaningful to write about and can find the time to maintain it every week. If you simply follow the leaders in your industry and rewrite what they have to say, you can position yourself as an authority. In some cases, you can gain positions in the search listings as your blog becomes a news item.

7. **Email marketing** - Absolutely NO. Companies in North America and Europe are flooded with spam emails from offshore companies every single day. There is no chance that a company getting hundreds of spam messages every day will answer any of those emails. Even if they had the interest, they wouldn't have the time. The only thing that will happen if you send these kinds of emails reaching out to employers is that you will be blocked and flagged by search engines and email providers. If companies remember your name from these spam emails, they will make a point of not hiring you in the future. Never use email marketing. You can email existing clients, assuming they don't ask you to remove them from your mailing list, but even then it is not recommended. If you choose to email existing clients, make sure you use an alternate email address. Otherwise, you risk having your personal or main work email reported as spam.

8. **Forum posts** - When used properly, forums can be effective. Don't spam forums or post with an obvious agenda. Engage the forum community and make real contributions. Ask informed questions and make comments that establish you as an authority. Once people recognize you as an authority, they will start to follow your posts, and may eventually ask if they can give you business. This is a long process without a guaranteed return. Remember how we discussed mastering your niche in Lesson 4? That is what you'll need to do to make forum posts work for you. You will need to be a master of your field and a valued source of knowledge in the forum community.

9. **Blog comments** - Absolutely NO. Blog comments are spam, and spam must be avoided at all costs. Nobody reacts well to spam, and if your name becomes associated with this kind of marketing, you will have a very hard time finding work.

10. **Phone Calls** - The answer depends on how you are intending to use phone calls. If you have something specific to offer the company you are calling, phone calls can work. For example, if you have a product or service that is

specifically made for dentists, then it makes sense to call dental offices to offer it. However, if you intend to make a more general call asking for work, then DO NOT DO IT. This is more spam. You will be dismissed along with the other calls Western employers get offering offshore website and marketing services every day.

Understand that marketing is based on statistics. If I advertise 100 times, 5 people will connect with me, and 1 will close a deal - a 100-to-1 relationship. Does the money I make from one deal pay for 100 ads? It's all about the numbers. Once you get your numbers right, you will really start to benefit.

Remember that you don't need many clients to have a great income. You only need a dedicated few that will send you work consistently, and then you're laughing all the way to the bank.

HOMEWORK:
1. List all of the marketing options that you are going to use.
2. Write in detail how you plan to advertise yourself, including the amount of time and money you intend to spend.

Lesson 8 - Money Management Practices

Everybody wants to talk about money, so let's get into it. I recommend these six money managing practices:

1. **Save your money -** The income of a freelancer is much less stable than some other jobs. There will be some months where you have many projects, and others where you have none. This is the nature of offshore work. Make sure that you keep some of the money that you generate in the "good months" aside to sustain you during the months where you have no projects. Don't spend all of your money when you get it.
2. **Use a milestone system -** When you are charging clients, it is very important that you do so according to a solid system of milestones. I recommend Escrow. Do the work on your server, and release it to the client's server as you proceed. Each goal or milestone that you create should be easy to test so that your client can quickly acknowledge the work has been done. Get written confirmation that each milestone has been achieved before you proceed. If you have reached your milestone and your client has not paid, you must stop working. Don't work for free - if they stop paying, you stop releasing work. You need to be upfront with your clients and tell them that you work hard to produce high-quality work, and in turn expect to be paid on time. You won't offend your employers by speaking in this way if you - it is very common where I come from, and Western employers won't take offence. Upload the finished project to the client's server only after receiving the final payment - I

have seen many cases where projects were loaded to the website before payment was received, and the developer was never paid. Don't let this happen to you!

3. **Use Escrow to attract new clients** - Getting new clients is hard. It takes time and money. When you're talking to a prospect whose project you feel you can complete, and you're sure you will do a great job, offer to accept payment through Escrow. Escrow is a trust third-party payment service that releases money in stages when terms agreed upon by both parties are met. This is an easy way to convince a client to say yes, since it is low-risk for both sides.

4. **Avoid the "Salami Attack"** - There is nothing more annoying for an employer than when a project keeps getting more expensive in "small increments" that seem to never end. I call it the "Salami Attack" - you keep buying small slices until eventually you've paid for the whole sausage. A project may start out costing $1,000, but then the developer will request more money due to small changes that arise beyond the scope of the original plan. Small changes to continue to add up, and before long the client is paying $2,000, and wondering why. Avoiding launching a surprise "Salami Attack" on your client, because there's nothing worst in their eyes. There is a better way. The first time you encounter a small change that needs to be made that falls outside the scope of the project you're working on, contact your client and tell them that you're willing to do it free of charge, but will need to charge for future out of scope changes. This will keep them happy. Once the second change is needed, contact the client and request a meeting. Ask him how he usually deals with changes that are beyond the scope of the original plan, as you do not feel comfortable adding charges every few days. If you approach the problem like this, your client will realize that you're on his side. Some clients will suggest paying extra at the end, some will prefer a monthly payment, and others will delay any additional items that arise beyond the scope of the original plan until phase 2 of the project (this is the prefered way). If the client asks you to propose a solution, you can offer any of these three options.

5. **Protect yourself from extra expenses** - From time to time, you'll need to buy extra fonts, plugins, themes, hosting, domains, SSL, etc. Make sure that the client is aware of these expenses as they happen, and let them pay these add-ons themselves. You don't want to take a loss on these if something goes wrong and you lose the project.

6. **Know how much to charge** - This is a common problem that offshore resources face. If you price your service too high, you lose the job because the client feels ripped off. If you price yourself too low, you lose the job because some clients associate "cheap" with "low-quality." It's best to aim for the middle; $7-$15 per hour is a good range to begin with. Give repeat clients a discount.

HOMEWORK:

1. Create a plan using each of the six money-managing practices listed in this section.
2. Read section 2 (Use a milestone system) few times and remember it.

Lesson 9 - Know Your Limit and Stay Within It

I often see offshore resources taking on more projects than they can handle. This is a very common problem, and it will kill your business over time.

Let's say that you have the time and energy to work on three projects at the same time. This is your maximum capacity or "comfort zone" - you know you can still do a good job and be on time with all three projects. Stay in your comfort zone at all times!

If you take on a fourth project in this scenario, all four will suffer. You will end up working endless hours and stressing day and night. Your work will be delayed and the quality will drop. Rather than delivering three great projects on time, you turn in four low-quality pieces of work behind schedule. Though you will get an extra "payday" from the fourth project, you will lose many more by turning in bad work. Good projects get you repeat business, while bad projects cost you money, clients, and quality of life.

Work within your limits, and good things will happen. Good work will get you referrals, whereas bad work can cost you all four paydays - is it really worth it?

HOMEWORK:
1. Calculate how many hours you are willing to work each day, and how many days you are able to work each week. Factor holidays and time off into your estimate. Based on that, build a working plan to see how many clients you would be able to serve. Make this a part of your working plan, and do not go over your limit.

Lesson 10 - Visualize the Perfect Project

In the past, I competed in professional martial arts competitions. As I prepared to compete, I would see myself fighting and winning. I would visualize the kicks I would throw, the feints I would use, how I would step to make my opponent miss - everything! I would see my hand raised and the crowd applauding my victory.

Once the fight came, it all very seemed familiar. I would execute the plan the way I imagined it. I achieved great results by taking the time to visualize the perfect match.

In order for you to succeed in your work, you will need to visualize as well. Imagine how a perfect project looks in your mind, and then work towards this goal.

This is how I imagine a great project going from my perspective as an experienced Canadian employer:

1. I post the outline for my project online to attract some talent.
2. I receive a few great resumes from offshore developers.
3. I conduct interviews, and notice that one resource (you!) stands out. This special offshore resource seems to know exactly what I'm looking for. After some small talk about my favourite sports team, he tells me that he is currently at his full capacity, but if we sign today, he will be able to start next week. I appreciate him being upfront, and respect that he cares about quality enough to limit the amount of projects he will take on at once. This special resource asks me questions about my company and the project, confirming all the details. I feel very comfortable with this employee, and decide to proceed with him.
4. Before we sign off on the project, the resource sends me a list of detailed milestones for the project. I can see that he understands my needs, and I am comfortable depositing money into an Escrow account.
5. The project begins a week later. I get an updates every day, whether it is a few words about what was done, or him informing me that there is something that I need to test. "What a positive change from my previous projects," I think. I love it!
6. On the day that a milestone is due, I get the result and it works perfectly. If there is a delay, I get a message from the resource a few days in advance with an honest explanation that makes sense to me. The resource also includes their plan to fix the problem in this message.
7. Before the project ends, the developer communicates with me and advises me on all I need to know for once it is launched. The resource gives me the source code, a thorough tutorial, and some troubleshooting advice to help me in the future.
8. After the project is launched, the developer connects with me to offer a few support plans. The support plans are very affordable, and keep me as a client for the long-term. I am happy to see that the support plan is not as expensive as some that I had to turn down in the past. I am amazed that the project ends neatly, with no hidden fees or hiccups. I am so impressed by my experience with this vendor.
9. The resource sends me a nice email once a month to keep in contact. The first one he writes reads: "Hello Lior, how are you? Just touching base. Any cool new projects I can help with this month?" It is pleasant, short, and helpful. If I ask him to stop sending me these emails, he stops immediately, not wanting to "spam" me.

As a Canadian employer, this is what I consider the perfect project. This is inside information, and is a rare opportunity for you to see exactly what your employer expects from you. You should provide this experience to your employer whenever possible.

Now that you know what to do, let me explain what NOT to do. I have had many projects go badly in my 15 years employing offshore resources. This is the kind of project experience you must avoid giving your employer at all costs:

1. I post the outline for my project online to attract some talent.
2. I receive a few great resumes from offshore developers.
3. Nobody stands out during the interview process. Every candidate promised me things that didn't seem true, and I did not feel as though any of their answers were "special." I have a bad feeling about this, but I have no choice but to take a risk with somebody. Eventually, I pick someone.
4. We sign on the project. The resource sends me a list of unclear milestones. I deposit the money with Escrow and keep a close watch on the process, expecting to have to ask for a refund at any moment.
5. The project starts, but I don't get any updates. I have to beg and chase my employee around for news and progress reports. I rarely get a reply. Communication is very poor, as with most of my offshore experiences.
6. When milestones are due, it feel like a lottery. There is a chance that I will get the result I am looking for, but I can only hope for the best. I am often disappointed. If there is a delay, I get no explanation, and am forced to chase them down to get a reason why the work is late. When I do finally hear back, I get the feeling that they're lying to me.
7. As the project wraps up, I get very little support from the developer. They are not advising me on what I need to do in order to launch the project, and I do not get any tutorial or walkthrough. No source code is provided to me. I have to pester the developer for these things to the point where I start to feel bad. I am working way more than I feel I should for the result I want, and I don't like it.
8. Once the project has launched, I either never hear from the offshore resource again, or they spam me non-stop with general marketing emails that I have no interest in. I request to be taken off of their mailing list, but the resource does not take action. I promise myself never to hire this person again.

I have described a good and bad project experience, from the perspective of the employer. It should be obvious which of these scenarios will generate more money and business for you in the future. If you want to succeed, visualize the perfect project, and deliver it to your employer!

HOMEWORK:
1. Referring to the employer expectations I have provided, create the perfect process for your business. Incorporate this perfect process into your business plan.

Lesson 11 - Testing

When a milestone deadline arrives, my resource will often send me work that is filled with bugs. I will spend time reviewing the work and identifying problem areas, then send the bug report to my resource. Once they have fixed the bugs I identified, the resource will send me another version. I will test the work again, identify other bugs, and send it back to be reworked. It might take 5 rounds of testing and revisions before the work is where it needs to be.

This is considered normal in the eyes of the offshore worker, but is not acceptable in the eyes of the employer. The entire reason that the employer is choosing to work with an offshore resource is to save time and money. If they have to test and revise the work being submitted 5 times before it is ready, he will quickly lose interest in working with you.

Think of it another way. When you walk into a store to buy a shirt, it is unacceptable for the store owner to ask you to test the product for small tears. Nobody wants to waste time spotting and repairing holes in a shirt they already bought!

In the same way, your employer expects a finished product if he has paid for it already. They will not be satisfied with something half-done.

However, you still need to test your work. How can you do this without disappointing your employer?

QA and testing services are very inexpensive solutions. They can be bought for about $3 per hour. During the interview and planning stages, offer your employer two options:

1. Charge them your hourly rate, with an extra $4 per hour set aside for any QA and testing that the project requires.
2. If the client doesn't want to use the third-party QA option, then tell them that they will need to do the testing themselves.

Note: Before you release a milestone you need to test your work at least twice. untested work in not acceptable!

Make sure your employer understand his options. Communication is key! As long as you explain the process and the need for testing to your employer, everything will be fine.

If your employer's hourly rate in his home country is $70 per hour, time spent testing will seem very expensive in his eyes. Imagine spending 10 hours on back-and-forth QA and testing every time a milestone deadline arrives! The cost will be huge.

If you offer your employer an inexpensive option, there is a very good chance that he will take it. You must offer this option early on in the process, ideally during the interview or planning stage before the deal is signed. If you offer this half way through the project, it will look like a "Salami Attack" as discussed in Lesson 8.

If you work as part of a team, you can help each other with testing and save a lot of money. Test your team member's work in exchange for having them test yours. The end result will be much better for both of you, and your efforts will go a long way towards fighting the reputation offshore workers have for providing low-quality work.

HOMEWORK:
1. Develop a solid plan to incorporate testing into your process. Find a teammate you can exchange testing work with, or research an inexpensive QA service. Your final goal is to make your clients happy, so create different options to suit different employers.

Lesson 12 - Referral Services

I want to see more referral services coming from offshore resources. If I require a service or skillset that my current offshore worker cannot provide, I don't want him to make an unqualified attempt that hurts my project. He will run into the problems I explained in Lesson 4. I will lose time and money, and our relationship will break down. Instead, I want him to connect me with someone qualified.

The right way to offer a referral is to look for high-quality companies or individuals whose services complement your own. This means that the company you choose will offer things you cannot provide. They will be a complement, not a competitor!

Close a written deal with this company that states any deal they close because of you earns you 10% per hour for as long as the project takes. Once you do this, you can refer clients and start making money for it without any liability if things go wrong.

When you make these referrals, it's important to tell your client that you have never worked with the company personally, but have heard good things. By doing so, you avoid making a guarantee that the resources you're recommending will be perfect. If something goes wrong, you will not be liable.

It's also important not to try to protect any company you recommend. If the client is not happy with the company, don't try to cover for them, and don't offer to check on them or find a solution. Stay away from their deal and remain neutral at all costs. If your client thinks that you are involved, then they will place the blame on you. You might lose your client as a result of their deal with another company going bad. If things go poorly, tell your client that you're sorry that they had a bad experience, and assure them that they can depart anytime.

HOMEWORK:

1. Locate quality offshore companies that you can work with in the future. The companies you choose should be in your industry, but should not offer the same services as you. Remember - the company should be a complement, not a competitor. For example, if you are a web developer proficient only in PHP, connect with companies who work only in .NET or graphic design.
2. Research legal agreements you can use to create terms for your referral services. A simple Google search will turn up many useful examples.

Lesson 13 - Trust

Trust is huge in the eyes of European and North American employers. Remember your "credit score" from lesson 1 - it was included in the opening section of this course for a reason!

Trust takes time to build and it is difficult to maintain. If you deliver good results on a few consecutive projects, your employer will begin to trust you. He will start sending you projects without interviewing your competitors, and will trust whatever price you give him.

At this point, you may feel as though trust is secured and your work is done, but that is not the case. You must continue to be completely loyal and honest. You can't charge more money than the project is worth. Don't assume that the client will stay with you forever and you can relax, either. It doesn't work that way - you must keep serving your client to the best of your ability, or you're lose the job and their trust.

Abusing trust is part of human nature. I saw it in every country and city I have ever worked in. I noticed vendors would start to give less and take more as I continued sending them work over time. Eventually, they would neglect our relationship so badly that I would have to end it.

If you want to be successful, you must protect your relationship with good clients in the same way you would protect your marriage. You have already spent hours finding good clients, so why throw them away? Your clients make it possible for you to pay for your house, food, car, and clothing. They deserve the best service possible, so don't abuse their trust.

HOMEWORK:

1. Modify your business plan as follows. Offer a special discount or bonus to any client who has 2 or more projects with you. This will strengthen your relationship, build trust, and increase the chances that the clients sends you more work.

Lesson 14 - Delays (and the problems they cause)

Delays are a big problem in business, and they're very common when working with offshore resources. In the following lesson, I discuss how delays look from the employer's perspective, and explain some of the problems they cause.

Let's assume that your client has a website that needs to be built. The client signs the deal with the developer, who says that the project will take 2 months to finish. This client is smart - he gives the developer a buffer in case of any delays, and tells his marketing company to expect the website in 3 months. The marketing company prepares a plan according to this schedule.

During the development stage, no problems are reported. Of course, this doesn't mean that there are no issues - many times the developer is simply afraid to upset their employer. Nevertheless, the client starts to buy banners, TV advertisements, and other media until everything is ready to advertise the new website.

When the project is scheduled to be uploaded to the production server, the client runs some tests and sees that the project is nowhere near being ready. A number of bugs are discovered, and few features and functions are missing.

The client meets with the developer, who promises that all of the problems will be solved within a week. One week later, more issues have been discovered. Before long, the 3-month deadline has arrived, and the website is still not ready.

Now, the client needs to cancel the marketing company service plan. Unfortunately, the deposit was already paid, so cancelling will cost him $15,000 with no return. The client is now losing momentum and missing big opportunities. He planned to have his website ready for the holidays, and is now unable to do so. The client spent a huge amount of money and wasted a big holiday sales opportunity, and it's quite likely that he will never recover from this loss.

If the project is ever completed, this employer will swear never to use offshore resources again. Sure, he saved $700 in labour, but he cost himself many sleepless nights, and over $15,000 in marketing fees! It's just not worth it.

Delays may seem like a small issue from your perspective as an employee, but they're not. An extra week's wait may seem very minor, but it can cost your employer everything. If you want to retain your clients and improve the reputation of offshore work, avoid delays at all costs!

HOMEWORK:

1. Create a list of projects that you have worked on, dividing the page in half to separate those that were on-time from those that missed were late. It is very common for offshore workers to have more items on the "late" side of the page, and this is a problem. All of your future projects will be written on the "on-time" side of the page, since missing deadlines is no longer an option.

Lesson 15 - Communications

Communication is key. There is no such thing as having "too much communication." More communication means less problems. The more time you spend speaking with the client, the more comfortable they will get with you. You will start to develop a connection, which benefits you both. You will each have very clear expectations, and there will be no nasty surprise when the product is finally delivered. You can avoid a lot of extra work fixing and rebuilding mistakes, and get many more jobs in the future.

In order to ensure that there is healthy communication between you and your employer, make sure that you do the following:

1. Start discussing the project's plan as early as the interview stage.
2. Discuss milestones as you are working through them.
3. Immediately seek clarification for any issues that you cannot solve on your own
4. If you feel that there is a better way to approach the project than the plan your client has proposed, offer your advice.
5. Give your client advanced notice if you anticipate any delays, and honestly explain why it happened.
6. Give your client advanced notice about any upcoming holidays or days off that you intend to take.
7. Give your client daily updates about the project. This is the key to good communication, and is an absolute requirement.

HOMEWORK:

1. Add to your business plan. Determine the "minimum" level of communication you will maintain with all clients. Keep in mind that each updates will only take a few minutes. As a general rule, contacting your client once per week should be the bare minimum.

Lesson 16 - Vacations

As an employer, there is nothing I hate more then when an offshore resource blindsides me by announcing a surprise holiday.

"Hi Lior, I just want to let you know that I am leaving tomorrow for a week-long holiday, and won't have much internet access while I'm away."

The project's deadline is in two weeks, and you're telling me this now? Surprising your employer like this is unacceptable. It wastes your employers' time and causes them problems with their clients.

Vacations must either be brought to your employer's attention well in advance, and factored into the timeline you provided during the first project meeting.

This issue can be avoided entirely if you follow Lessons 14 and 15. As you can see, the lessons in this course fit together like the pieces of a puzzle. If you follow this guide carefully, you eliminate most of the problems offshore workers face.

HOMEWORK:

1. Make a note in your business plan to inform all clients about your upcoming vacations or holidays, and to factor these trips into the timelines that you give clients.

Lesson 17 - Working Hours

Time zone differences make working hours a big problem for many offshore workers. When you are 7+ hours behind or ahead of your employer, it can be very easy to miss deadlines.

There is a way to avoid delays and missed deadlines caused by time differences. Propose to your employer that you will arrange your working hours so that there is an "overlap" between the time you two work.

In some cases, your employer will need your help in real-time. He will need you to be "live" during meetings, or before uploading a new project. You may need to stay up a little later or wake up a bit earlier, but it will be worth it to keep your client happy.

In my experience, projects cannot succeed without this "overlap." If you cannot interact with your employer in real-time, your project will fail. Spending all of your time looking for new employers is not profitable or productive, so you must make sure that you keep your projects alive by coordinating your working hours.

HOMEWORK:

1. Make a note in your business plan to overlap working hours with your employer. What will be the minimum amount of hours you overlap with your client? You can calculate this number per day or per week.

Lesson 18 - Thinking Outside the Box

Clients may be excellent business people, but that doesn't mean they know much about your specific area of expertise - that is often why they're hiring you to do the work, after all. There will be times during your project when your client makes an ignorant request that shows their lack of understanding in your field.

For example, your client might request that you build a blog website. He suggests using a custom system that will cost about $10,000 to develop. In your mind, you know right away that this is a mistake. The client could get the same results with a $500 WordPress site, so why not suggest that? The client will be happy with the solution and the chance to save so much money, and it will save you a lot of work as well.

Don't blindly follow your client's instructions. They do not always know what they are talking about, and will rely on your expertise to guide them down the right path. Don't be afraid to propose a different solution that will work better.

When you propose an alternate solution, make sure that you say it in a very nice and professional manner. For example, you might say: "Your idea good. Can I offer you an alternative that many people have not heard of? It could save you a lot of money." This allows you to offer an alternative while you acknowledge the employer's suggestion as valid.

HOMEWORK:
1. Make a note in your business plan to propose clients alternatives in case their idea is not best practice.

Lesson 19 - Copyrights

Many offshore developers, designers, marketers, and content writers are guilty of ignoring copyright laws. Offshore resources do this because it makes their job easier, and they understand that these laws won't be enforced against them. Obviously, a New York lawyer won't come to India to sue you, but he will come after your client. Don't expect to get work from this ever again client if that happens.

When you use pictures, music, videos, and other content, you need to make sure that it's unique, or free to use. If you find a website that hosts royalty-free content, make sure you take a screenshot of the page where this is stated. Send this screenshot to the client, and keep a copy of your own incase anybody tries to claim the content violates copyright law.

Copyright is a huge problem that offshore workers have to deal with these days. Developers have specifically web-crawlers whose only purpose is to detect copyright. Once copyright violation has been detected, blood-thirsty lawyers will pounce and try to get as much money out of you (or your client) as possible. I was personally involved in a case where a competitor stole pictures and content from my website. I sued him for $500,000, and though I did not win the full amount, I did receive a large sum.

HOMEWORK:

1. Make a list of royalty-free websites in your business plan and categorize them for easy usage.

Final Thoughts:

Thank you for taking this course!

The topic of offshore work is very close to my heart. I see the offshore workforce as the single greatest opportunity being overlooked in our time.

I am very distressed by the negative migration away from offshore hiring, especially since most of the problems could be solved if the expectations of Western employers were explained in full. After seeing and experiencing this problem for many years, I finally decided to take the time to create this course.

In turn, I hope that you take the time to study these lessons in full. Once you have finished this program, you will have developed a strong business plan that is built to succeed in the Western world. The knowledge you will have gained with this course will help you stand out from the competition, and transform you into a special resource that Western employers will not want to pass up.

Good luck!

www.ingramcontent.com/pod-product-compliance
Lightning Source LLC
Chambersburg PA
CBHW082305200526
45168CB00018B/3420